Spanish   *Junior*
Memory   *Edition*
Book

Spanish Memory Book

A NEW APPROACH TO VOCABULARY BUILDING

Junior Edition

BY WILLIAM F. HARRISON AND
DOROTHY WINTERS WELKER

ILLUSTRATIONS BY ANITA NELSON

University of Texas Press *Austin*

Library of Congress Cataloging-in-Publication Data

Harrison, William F., 1934–
    Spanish memory book : a new approach to vocabulary build-
ing / by William F. Harrison and Dorothy Winters Welker ;
illustrations by Anita Nelson. — Junior ed., 1st ed.
        p.   cm.
    Summary: Provides mnemonic devices for committing about
350 Spanish words to memory.
    ISBN 0-292-73079-9 (alk. paper). — ISBN 0-292-73081-0
(pbk. : alk. paper)
    1. Spanish language—Vocabulary.   [1. Spanish language—
Vocabulary.]   I. Welker, Dorothy Winters, 1905– .
II. Nelson, Anita C., 1949–   ill.   III. Title.
PC4445.H37   1993
468.1—dc20   93-12717

Contents

To the Reader

In learning a new language, one of your first goals is to acquire a large stock of useful words in that language. The *Spanish Memory Book, Junior Edition,* is designed to help you learn Spanish words easily and fast and to recall them at will. It will enable you to recognize Spanish words when you see or hear them (passive vocabulary), and to recall these words when you speak or write Spanish (active vocabulary).

The *Spanish Memory Book, Junior Edition,* accomplishes this by means of mnemonic devices (memory helps). Mnemonic devices are not new, of course. They have been used for centuries. We still call upon them every day to remember names, numbers, and many others things: "*Spring* forward in the *spring, fall* back in the *fall.*" The mnemonic device sets up an association between a new word and old words that enables us to recall the new word. The mnemonic devices used in the *Spanish Memory Book* are rhymes that help you to remember both the pronunciation of the Spanish words and their English meanings. They fairly jingle the new words into your memory.

Research has shown, surprisingly enough, that the more far-fetched, even absurd, a mnemonic device is, the better it helps you remember. You will probably agree that many of the jingles in the *Spanish Memory Book* qualify for high marks in absurdity. You will have a good time learning and applying them.

The *Spanish Memory Book* contains about 250 words, which were selected (with a half-dozen exceptions) from the two thousand most useful words in Spanish.*

*These words are listed in order of usefulness in the *Graded Spanish Wordbook,* compiled by Milton A. Buchanan, 3d ed., Toronto: University of Toronto Press, 1941.

How to Use the Spanish Memory Book

Read the Spanish entry and the corresponding jingle, for example:

bailar   *to dance*

<u>**Buy lar**</u>ger shoes *to dance* in.
Buy smaller pants to prance in.

The word to be learned is ***bailar,*** English "to dance." Incorporated in the jingle is a consecutive series of English sounds that resemble the sounds of Spanish ***bailar.*** These sounds are ***buy lar,*** and are underscored. Say the underscored syllables carefully, making sure you pronounce them exactly as you pronounce them in the English word. Then note the corresponding English words ("to dance"), which are also incorporated in the jingle and which are set in bold italics.

    Now look away from the book and ask yourself, What is the English word for ***bailar?*** Chances are you will come up at once with "to dance." If not, just read the jingle once more.

Shall we do another word?

dedo   *toe*

Each **day, though** chased by hordes of mice,
We search our grimy *toes* for lice.

Here English *day though* gives the sound of Spanish
dedo. The English equivalent is "toe."
    And here is one more. Do it on your own.

punto   *point*

When Ben's har**poon to**re up the joint
I guess the owner got the *point.*

Conventions Used in This Book

1. The jingles approximate as closely as possible the sounds and stresses of the Spanish words. When exactitude is not possible, the Spanish syllables are approximated. For the fine points of pronunciation, turn to a Spanish textbook or to your Spanish teacher. A table of pronunciations is provided in this book as a convenient reference.

2. The English equivalent of the Spanish word may appear in a jingle in any convenient form. For example, a verb may be in any tense. A noun may be either singular or plural. The main Spanish entry (alphabetical) always gives the infinitive of verbs and the singular of nouns.

3. The gender of nouns is given, except for nouns ending in *o*, which are usually masculine, or in *a*, usually feminine. Endings are given for adjectives that indicate gender by *o* and *a.*

4. To make possible the inclusion of many Spanish words containing the sound *a* (English h*o*t, f*a*ther),

the **Memory Book** occasionally replaces this sound by one of two similar sounds: ə (English *a*bout) or ɔ (English c*au*ght). This liberty has been taken only in unstressed syllables.

Note: The **Memory Book** is aimed primarily at helping you learn vocabulary. It cannot give conjugations of verbs, rules of sentence structure, or fine points of pronunciation. To do so would reduce the number of words that could be included and would encroach on the territory of language teachers and of grammar and linguistics textbooks.

Pronunciation

This section is included to serve as a reference in case you have occasion to refer to the basic rules of Spanish pronunciation.

VOWELS* AND DIPHTHONGS

Spanish	English Approximation
a	*a* in father
ai/all/ay	*eye*
au	t*ow*n
e	t*a*ke
ei/ell/ey	w*ei*gh; similar to Spanish *e*, but longer
i	mach*i*ne
io/yo	*yo*ke
o	n*o*
oi/oll/oy	b*oy*
u	S*u*san; silent between *g* and *i*, between *g* and *e,* and after *q*

*Spanish single vowel sounds are always short and tense.

uo	*woe*
ua	sq*ua*t
ue	*way*

CONSONANTS

Spanish	English Approximation
b/v	*b*anana at the beginning of a sentence or of a word-group within a sentence, and after *m* or *n;* elsewhere the lips barely meet.
c	*c*at before *a, o, u,* or a consonant; *s*at before *i* or *e*
ch	*ch*art
d	*d*og at the beginning of a sentence or of a word-group within a sentence, and following *n* or *l;* elsewhere *d* approximates the *th* in *th*ey
f	*f*in
g	*g*o before *a, o, u;* strongly aspirated *h* before *i* and *e*
h	always silent
j	strongly aspirated *h*
l	*l*ittle
ll	*y*es; *all* is pronounced *aye*
m	*m*other
n	like English *n* except preceding *m, b,* and *v,* when it is pronounced *m*
ñ	ca*ny*on

p	s*p*y
q	*q* is always followed by silent *u;* the combination is pronounced like *k* in *k*ite
r	after *n* and *l* and at the beginning of a word *r* is trilled, resulting in a sound something like the one children produce in imitating a motor; elsewhwere *r* approximates the *tt* in po*tt*y
rr	always trilled
s	*s*o
t	*t*ask
x	soc*ks;* in a few Indian words such as México and Oaxaca *x* is pronounced like a strongly aspirated *h*
y	*y* in *y*es; when *y* stands alone it approximates the *e* in *e*qual
z	*s*o

Spanish   *Junior*
Memory   *Edition*
Book

Vocabulary

Aa

acá   *here*

Ah, calm my puppy. Set him down right *here,*
So he can yelp for joy when I appear.

acera   *sidewalk*

Ah, Sarah, keep the *sidewalk* neat.
Walk your dog along the street.

acero   *steel*

Ah, say romantic words you really feel,
And learn to bend a bit, O man of *steel.*

acoger   *to harbor, greet, receive*

P**a, coher**ence is a virtue.
Harbor it. It will not hurt you.

adiós   *good-bye*

Ah! the oh so lovely child!
She said *good-bye* and sweetly smiled.

acera *sidewalk*

Ah, Sarah, keep the *sidewalk* neat.
Walk your dog along the street.

afuera   *outside*

Take your coat <u>**off, wear a**</u> sweater.
It's warm *outside,* but getting wetter.

agrícola   *agricultural*

We <u>**agree cola**</u>'s truly a boon
On a hot *agricultural* noon.

ahorrar   *to save*

P<u>**a or Ar**</u>t must *save* and scrimp
To get our Ma some out-sized shrimp.

ajo   *garlic*

<u>**Ah, Jo**</u>sé, once more I say:
"*Garlic* scares the girls away."

alcanzar   *to reach (a place)*

At last the B<u>**alkan ser**</u>geant *reached* his goal,
But never could pronounce Sebastopol.

alce (m.)   *moose, elk*

I just don't know what M<u>**a'll say**</u>
   when we bring home the *moose.*
And when she hears his banjo,
   I fear she'll turn him loose.

alegre   *happy, merry*

A leg Ray is *happy* to bare
Is tattooed with the head of his mare.

alemán (m.)   *German*

All a monocled *German* can think of to do
Is to stare out of one eye and not out of two.

alguno, -a   *some*

All goon? No way! *Some* say it's so,
But Herman's only dull and slow.

alimentar   *to feed*

Ollie meant Arthur *to feed* her pet cat,
But Arthur likes cat food, the treacherous brat.

almacén (m.)   *store*

Alma sent me to the *store*.
But I forgot to ask what for.

altivo, -a   *proud, haughty*

M**oll, T-bo**ne steaks attract our crowd,
And yet for stew we're not too *proud*.

alto, -a   *high, tall*

M**oll to**ld Mary she still feels quite spry,
But as for jumping, finds the fence too *high*.

amarillo, -a *yellow*

Ah, Marie, Yolanda's turning *yellow*
Because she's eaten too much lemon Jello.

amo *landlord*

T**om, mo**lasses makes the cookies snappy.
We'll give the *landlord* some to keep him happy.

amor (m.) *love*

A mortal wholly lacking *love*
Is like a hand without a glove.

ancho, -a *wide*

The swamp that P**ancho** tried to pass
Is *wide* and full of deadly gas.

andén (m.) *platform*

The railroad *platform* fell **on Den**ny.
It injured him and frightened many.

aniversario *anniversary*

L**onnie, bear sorry o**ld Artie
To his last *anniversary* party.

anotar *to write down*

P**a, no tar**nish stains your knightly sword.
Your race will *write* this *down:* "He served the Lord."

apagar   *to turn off*

Our p<u>apa guar</u>ds his children's health
And *turns off* lights to save their wealth.

aparejar   *to rig, prepare*

<u>**Ah, Pa, Ray har**</u>dly ever tries *to rig*
The sailboat; he's too bunglesome and big.

apio   *celery*

C<u>opy o</u>nly a *celery* stalk.
Stand up straight and just don't talk.

apreciar   *to appreciate*

<u>**Ah, pray C.R.**</u> *appreciates*
The pains you take to keep your dates.

aprender   *to learn*

A t<u>op wren dare</u>s, no doubt, *to learn*
To fly to France when it comes her turn.

apretar   *to squeeze*

P<u>**a, pray tar**</u> and feather those
Who *squeeze* us into small-sized clothes.

arco   *bow (weapon)*

H<u>ark, O</u> gentle Cupid. Bend your *bow,*
But aim no arrows at the girls I know.

arma   *gun, arm, weapon*

We'll **arm a** nation with tanks and ships
And pile up *guns* till the enemy flips.

asco   *repugnance, nausea*

M**a sco**lds Father for his strange
Repugnance to the laws of change.

así   *thus, so*

Ah, see the rapidly approaching bus.
It may not stop if you keep screaming *thus.*

asistir   *to attend, be present*

Hurr**ah! See steer**s *attend* the meeting.
Hear the cows all low their greeting.

asomar   *to come into view, begin to appear*

Ah, so marvelous it was—on cue
The Stars and Stripes *came* floating *into view.*

atentamente   *politely*

A tent o' men takes patience to awaken.
They must be firmly but *politely* shaken.

atroz   *atrocious*

Wh**at roas**t can equal that of venison?
(But it's *atrocious* if it's overdone.)

alce (m.)   *moose, elk*

I just don't know what M**a'll say**
   when we bring home the ***moose***.
And when she hears his banjo,
   I fear she'll turn him loose.

aula *classroom*

H**owl a**way! You merit your fate.
You must clean the **classroom** because you're late.

aunque *though, although*

Though loved by all the t**own, Kay** has a quirk:
She tends to go to sleep while others work.

aurora *dawn*

N**ow roar a**while, and get it off your chest.
When comes the ***dawn,*** you'll find your ma knows best.

ave (f.) *bird*

Rely on my word: B**ob a**te our ***bird.***
You say he's a bird-lover? Simply absurd!

avestruz *ostrich*

Ah, Bess! Truces recently were signed
Between the ***ostriches*** and all mankind.

aviso *ad, advertisement*

I know **a bee so** bold he thought it funny
To answer someone's ***ad*** for homemade honey.

ayuno *fast* (n.)

Aye, you know how to keep a solemn ***fast:***
You make your sailors tie you to the mast.

azúcar (m.)   *sugar*

A Sioux careened into yonder shelf,
Opened the *sugar,* and helped himself.

azul   *blue*

A Sioux'll be there when the fun begins,
Wearing his *blue* fur moccasins.

Bb

bailar   *to dance*

Buy larger shoes to *dance* in;
Buy smaller pants to prance in.

bajar   *to get off, descend*

Dear old Ab**ba har**dly made a sound
When, tottering, he *got off* the merry-go-round.

bajo, -a   *low, short*

—My score was *low* on the medical test.
—**Bah! Ho**me remedies work out best.

barba   *beard*

A **barba**rous practice, greatly feared,
Is shaving off a convict's *beard.*

basto, -a   *coarse, homespun*

Bah! Stone tools are *coarse* and out of date,
So tell the salesman that he needn't wait.

beber   *to drink*

Give the **babe air,** make her *drink* water.
After all, boys, she's somebody's daughter.

bien   *fine, well*

The season would **be en**ding *fine*
If you would be my valentine.

bobo, -a   *foolish, silly*

Bo, Bohemian party pooper,
Is *foolish,* but his grins are super.

bocado   *bite, mouthful*

This dra**b oak, ah!, though** stung by blight,
Still yields my horse a leafy *bite.*

bonito, -a   *pretty*

—Is Ram**bo neat, o**r slightly nutty?
—He's just a *pretty* piece of putty.

bueno, -a   *good*

Though you, Bo**b, weigh no** more than Jim,
Your *good* karate vanquished him.

buey (m.)   *ox, bull, steer*

The su**bway** must be on the rocks:
This train is powered by an *ox.*

busca   *search*

Let's end the futile *search* for "maybe's"
    and "perhapses,"
And plan what we can do when this
    ca<u>**boose co**</u>llapses.

buscar   *to seek, look for*

Bam<u>**boo scar**</u>s are mostly not too serious.
But *seek* a doctor if you get delirious.

Cc

cabeza   *head*

—Don't let the In**ca base a** camp
Here where the ground is cold and damp.
His *head* will ache, his legs will cramp.
—Don't worry. He's a hardy scamp.

cabra   *goat*

The **cob Ra**mona cooked for Henry's dinner
Was eaten by a *goat.* So he got thinner.

cadena   *chain*

Dor**ca, they kno**cked out the thief.
Now he's in *chains;* so what's your beef?

caer   *to fall*

The In**ca er**ror was, they stopped to yell
When Rabbit-in-the-Moon, their leader, *fell.*

caja   *box*

Loo**k! ah, ho**t coffee! And a *box*
Of the very best quality kosher lox!

calcetín (m.)   *sock*

All the books of proto**col say teen**s
Should pull their *socks* up when they're wearing jeans.

campo   *field, campus*

The **compo**st heap you put in yonder *field*
Offends the nose, but will increase our yield.

cantar   *to sing*

Jane's smiles **con Tar**zan into *singing*
And start his great gorillas swinging.

canto   *song*

When **Kahn to**bogganed down that hill,
His tuneless *song* was sounding still.

capaz   *capable*

Foolish Dor**ca, pos**turing and prancing,
Believes she's *capable* of modern dancing.

cara   *face*

My **car a**gain has lost a race.
It just exploded in my *face.*

cárcel (f.)   *jail*

Those who from a **car sell** drugs
Must go to *jail* like other thugs.

cargo   *load, burden*

I watched our **car go** limping with its *load.*
It almost capsized when it hit a toad.

carne (f.)   *meat*

—The **car Na**te sold me smells of rancid *meat.*
—He once sold spicy hot dogs on the street.

carrera   *race*

Dic**k, a rare a**ttempt has just been made
To stage a rat *race* in the second grade.

comer   *to eat*

Bas**com, heir** to Grandpa's wealth,
Ate all day and wrecked his health.

cometer   *to commit*

Comb a terrorist and find a sadist.
Of all bad actions, he *commits* the baddest.

comida   *meal*

I'm no co-worker. I'm just **co-me.**
The *meals* I like are the ones served free.

contestar   *to answer, reply*

—**Cohn, test Ar**thur's readiness *to answer.*
—I've done so, and he stammers what he can, sir.

contra   *against*

The ice-cream **cone tra**versed a ten-inch gap
And crashed *against* the Flight Commander's lap.

correr   *to run*

Core rare ripe apples for the table,
But *run* with green ones to the stable.

cuenta   *bill, account*

Jac**k went a**-fishing in the ocean,
Brought back a *bill* for suntan lotion.

cuerpo   *body*

A s**quare po**sition is the best
To give your battered *body* rest.

Dd—Ee

dar   *to give*

Darla, *give* to Tom your best,
And leave to others all the rest.

dedo   *finger, toe*

Each **day, though** chased by hordes of mice,
We search our grimy *toes* for lice.

dejar   *to leave (behind), allow*

Some **day har**m will come to those
Who *leave* unwashed their underclothes.

delito   *crime*

One **day Lee to**ld all about his *crime.*
Now he must stand his trial and serve his time.

desear   *to want, desire, wish*

The boys each **day say ar**dent prayers:
They *want* to meet the girl upstairs.

desprecio   *disdain, contempt*

Dess, pray see over the hedge and down the lane
A moose observing us all with high *disdain.*

día (m.)   *day*

New i**dea**s hit me every *day.*
Sometimes I almost wish they'd go away.

dirigir   *to steer, direct*

Deary, hear me when I plead:
Steer the boat but watch your speed.

disculpar   *to excuse*

Dee, school parties don't *excuse*
Your cutting class to take a snooze.

dormir   *to sleep*

THIS **door mere**ly leads to the castle keep.
Our ghost lives there to haunt you while you *sleep.*

enfermo, -a   *sick, ill*

Wh**en fair Mo**desta's dog was *sick*
He sought his mistress' hand to lick.

escalar   *to scale, climb*

B**ess, call Ar**t *to scale* the wall.
We'll get out now or not at all.

feliz   *happy*

I'm *happy* that the tree **fell east**.
It killed an Oriental beast.

fiar   *to guarantee, sell on credit, trust*

When Du**ffy ar**gues loud and long
I *guarantee* that he'll be wrong.

fiel   *faithful, loyal*

The *faithful* Du**ffy, el**egant and loyal,
Defends the flag on his ancestral soil.

figura   *figure, countenance, shape*

The ta**ffy goo Ra**mona often ate
Enlarged her *figure* to a forty-eight.

flota   *fleet*

The ship will **float a** while and then go down.
The *fleet* has lost the jewel in its crown.

freno　　　　　　*brake*

Re**frain, O** driver, from grabbing the **brake,**
Or we'll end up in the nearest lake.

fundar　　　　　　*to base, found*

Where once a ty**phoon dar**kened sky and sea
We **based** our camp with glamor, guts, and glee.

gema　　　　　　*egg yolk*

Hey, Ma**cCarthy! Keep on cracking jokes!
We'll pay with a barrage of goose-**egg yolks!**

gente (f.)　　　　*people*

O **hen, ta**ke care! Avoid mishaps.
Don't lay your eggs in *people*'s laps.

gordo, -a　　　　*fat*

Gre**gor, though** *fat,* can woo and win.
I love him whether fat or thin.

gorra　　　　　　*cap*

That lady breeds an**gora** cats.
She treats them like aristocrats,
And gives them yellow *caps* and spats
To brighten up their habitats.

gota   *drop*

Go, Tom, get a kitchen mop.
On my floor you've spilled a *drop.*

gozo   *joy*

I wish our driver wouldn't **go so** fast.
It kills my *joy* and leaves me all aghast.

gritar   *to shout, scream*

Greet Tarzan climbing down the tree.
Just *shout* and *scream,* and so will he.

guía (f. and m.)   *guide*

Mc**Gee a**ppears to need a *guide*
Through this uncharted countryside.

Hh

haber   *to have* (aux.)

Ah, bury the hatchet! Be we right or wrong,
We two *have* heard again love's old sweet song.

hasta   *until, all the way to*

The p**asta** sitting on my plate
Was good *until* I overate.

helar   *to freeze*

It's quite **a lar**k, I found, to skate on ice,
But if you *freeze* your toes it's not so nice.

hender   *to split*

End Eric's urge to pose and prance
I laughed so hard I *split* my pants.

hermano   *brother*

The two little *brothers* just won't get dressed.
They've got to learn that th**eir ma know**s best.

hilar   *to spin*

<u>Bee, lar</u>cenous as ever, *spun* a yarn
About a treasure buried in a barn.

hombre (m.)   *man*

This learned <u>tome, bra</u>ve *man,* relates your story;
But does not name the price you paid for glory.

hotel (m.)   *hotel*

<u>Oh, tel</u>l me what unholy spell
Has drawn you to the Grand *Hotel!*

hueco   *gap, hole*

<u>Wake, O</u> master, lest there be no *gap*
Between your a.m. and your p.m. nap.

huerto   *garden, orchard*

Are you a<u>ware to</u>matoes crack and harden
If they are left unwatered in the *garden?*

hueso   *bone*

Don't throw a<u>way so</u> many scraps,
But scrape the *bones* to bait our traps.

huída   *flight, escape*

<u>We the</u> people think we're right,
So all our foes should take to *flight.*

humano, -a   *human*

Look y<u>ou, Ma, no *human*</u> mind can know
Where stars are born or clouds and comets go.

húmedo, -a   *humid, damp*

Wh<u>o **may tho**</u>se intrepid fellows be
Who camp in ***humid*** caverns by the sea?

Ii–Jj

ir   *to go*

The words you lavish on my brother
Go in one <u>ear</u> and out the other.

istmo   *isthmus*

From West to <u>**East Moe**</u> sped across the *Isthmus,*
Inviting all the kiddies here for Christmas.

jamás   *never*

<u>**Ha! Mos**</u>cow, *never* yet a place to go,
Last summer shed its ill repute like snow.

jefe (m.)   *chief, boss*

<u>**Hey, Fe**</u>licia, call the *chief.*
He'll put handcuffs on this thief!

junco   *junk (a Chinese ship)*

Cal<u>**houn, co**</u>-owner of my Chinese *junk,*
Is munching fortune cookies in his bunk.

Ll–LLll

ley (f.) *law*

Lay down the *law,* sir, as you please,
But no one tells me when to sneeze.

libra *pound*

Sara **Lee brou**ght home a *pound* of butter
When what we needed was a paper cutter.

libre *free*

Lee, brave men like you, if right or wrong,
Have helped to keep our country *free* and strong.

loco, -a *insane, mad*

This **loco**motive seems to be *insane,*
Snorting and snarling like a bull in pain.

lucha *fight*

Lou chops up his meat so small,
He doesn't need to chew at all.
But just involve him in a *fight,*
You'll find the chap knows how to bite.

luchar   *to struggle, fight*

<u>**Lou char**</u>red the steak, and how we hate it!
We had *to struggle,* but we ate it.

llamar   *to call*

Chuck will tell <u>**ya mar**</u>velous old stories.
Call him in to paint our former glories.

Mm

mal   *badly*

Ma'll be *badly* hurt to see
Her daughter lose the spelling bee.

maleta   *suitcase*

Ma**ma, late a**rriving from vacation,
Lost her *suitcase* at the railroad station.

manera   *way, manner*

"In some *ways,* boys I know," said Sarah,
"Don't quite belong in the hu**man era**."

mano (f.)   *hand*

Ma, no one but you will understand
The need I sometimes feel to hold your *hand.*

manto   *cloak, mantle*

A rare Ver**mont to**rnado tore his *cloak,*
But Nemo stood as steadfast as an oak.

mareo   *dizzy spell, dizziness*

—Is O<u>mar A.O.</u>K.? Do tell!
—Yes, he's over his *dizzy spell.*

martes (m.)   *Tuesday*

On *Tuesday* every local artist
Tries to show that he's the s<u>martes</u>t.

marzo   *March*

Breezes <u>**mar so**</u> the month of *March*
Our skirts are losing all their starch.

más   *more*

<u>**Ma, s**</u>et out our usual meal:
More beans and bacon, no big deal.

masa   *dough*

<u>**Ma, Sa**</u>mantha's always kneading *dough,* so
Why are her tortillas only so-so?

mascar   *to chew*

<u>**Ma scar**</u>red her costly lower plate
By *chewing* hard on what she ate.

mecer   *to swing, rock*

<u>**May cer**</u>emonies always bring
That keen desire to sway and *swing!*

menos   *less*

Dick considers **May no s**illy fool.
She's *less* than eager, though, to go to school.

miedo   *fear (n.)*

She gave **me A, though** I looked for a B.
My *fear* is, I deserved a C.

miel (f.)   *honey*

Trust **me, El**lie. I'll get money
Soon as I can sell our *honey.*

mil   *thousand*

A *thousand* hot dogs at a **meal**!
For elephants it's no big deal.

moda   *fashion*

Mow the lawn with pain and passion.
Keep your flower beds in *fashion.*

modo   *way*

Moe, though bashful, got his *way,*
For every dog must have his day.

mono   *monkey*

Moan no more that your *monkey*'s dead.
I'll give you a talking bird instead.

mil   *thousand*

A *thousand* hot dogs at a <u>**meal!**</u>
For elephants it's no big deal.

mozo   *waiter, boy*

Moe so resented the flies in his stew
That he called on the *waiter* to swallow a few.

mucho, –a   *much*

I hope a **moo cho**kes all your cattle.
Much lowing makes my brains just rattle.

mudo, –a   *mute, silent*

S**mooth o**ld feuds by playing on your flute,
And end each fight by simply staying *mute.*

mundo   *earth, world*

Look at the **moon. Do**n't ask me why
It follows the *earth* around the sky.

muro   *wall*

The old men **moor o**ld sailboats close to shore,
Sit on the *wall,* and talk of days of yore.

museo   *museum*

Moose, say O.K. to the truth I taught you:
You can't leave town. The *museum* bought you.

Nn–Oo

nadie   *no one*

Nah! The apes in zoos won't bite your finger.
In fact, they grieve when *no one* wants to linger.

natación (f.)   *swimming*

It's **not a sea, on**ly a sort of puddle.
But *swimming* will give us a chance to cuddle.

nombre (m.)   *name*

The g**nome, bra**ve fellow, drab and dumpy,
Gravely said his *name* was Grumpy.

nunca   *never*

At **noon Ka**tinka *never* ate a bite.
But she came home at five and gorged all night.

océano   *ocean*

Oh, say a no to *ocean* travel!
From this time on we stick to gravel.

ocho   *eight*

M**oe cho**ked over his *eight*-ball game,
Turned to golf but did the same.

ola   *wave*

Bob st**ole a** wigwam from a brave.
Were he a fish he'd steal a *wave!*

olvidar   *to forget*

C**olby, thar** she blows! But don't *forget*
A killer whale will never make a pet.

oprimir   *to press, oppress*

Why *press* me for the meaning of "pre-war"?
You surely kn**ow "pre" mere**ly means "before."

otro   *other, another*

The c**oat Ro**berto chanced to purchase at a sale
Outlasted all his *others,* for it's a coat of mail.

pagar   *to pay*

Pa, Garfinkel *pays* all his doctor bills,
But just won't take those nasty headache pills.

palabra   *word*

—I can't get this door open. How absurd!
—**Poll, abra**cadabra is the magic *word.*

pálido, –a   *pale*

Polly, though she's weak and *pale,*
Is good at bringing in the mail.

para   *in order to, for*

Pa robbed little Ernie's piggy bank
In order to pursue some silly prank.

parar   *to stop*

Gas**par, are** you now a traffic cop?
I fear you've learned to go, but not *to stop.*

patinar   *to skate*

<u>Pa, teen ar</u>guments aren't so nice.
They leave you *skating* on thin ice.

pedir   *to ask, ask for, request*

<u>Pay th' eer</u>ie creature half a dollar.
But *ask* him bluntly not to holler.

pelar   *to pluck, pull out (hair)*

<u>Pale ar</u>mies haunted me all night.
I *plucked* my hairs out, stiff with fright.

pelea   *fight*

<u>Pelé, a</u> champion player of soccer,
Has started a terrible *fight* at his locker.

peligro   *danger*

I'll <u>**pay Lee gro**</u>ss sums to keep this stranger
From putting me and those I love in *danger.*

peor   *worse*

In spring **pay or**dinarily is more.
But mine's *worse* this month than it was before.

pequeño, -a   *little, small*

"We must **pay Kane,**" **Yo**landa muttered sadly,
"Or he may hurt our *little* business badly."

perder   *to lose*

Pare <u>THEIR</u> ripe fruit, but leave MY apple whole.
Who scorns the skin *has lost* the apple's soul.

perezoso, -a   *lazy*

Pare <u>a so-so</u> fruit, and you may find
Lazy insects have already dined.

pero   *but*

Put him on the **payro**ll, *but*
Don't forget the guy's a nut.

perro   *dog*

We saw two figures struggling through the fog.
The **pair o**'ertook us—Buster and his *dog*.

picar   *to prick, sting*

The hap**py car**load, munching Fritos,
Were pricked each moment by mosquitoes.

pie (m.)   *foot*

Snoo**py A**da spied once more—
Caught her *foot* in my back door.

pintor   *painter*

No, Po**p, e'en tor**ture won't unlock the *painter*'s lips.
He won't say why for still-life scenes he uses paper clips.

pluma   *pen*

The **plume a**ppeared as mankind's only *pen.*
All you had to do was pluck a hen.

polvo   *dust*

Poll Bo's playmates. Can they, if they must,
First wield a tomahawk, then bite the *dust?*

poner   *to set, place*

Corn **pone ne'er** requires a label.
Just *set* it steaming on the table.

porque   *because*

I rate **pork A**-1 to cook *because*
It has no fur, no feathers, fuzz, or claws.

poste (m.)   *pillar, pole, post*

After you **post a** bond, though not a killer,
You'll find your photo mounted on a *pillar.*

postre (m.)   *dessert*

Post tray-bearing waiters in the aisles,
To pass *dessert* with festive bows and smiles.

pozo   *well, pit*

Folks dro**p oh! so** many pennies into the wishing *well,*
But ah! how many brought them luck what sorcerer
    can tell?

prever   *to anticipate, foresee*

<u>**Pray bear**</u> with me, and just *anticipate*
You'll find me always slow, and sometimes late.

previo, –a   *previous, prior*

<u>**Pray be o**</u>pen to my suggestion.
At least, reply to my *previous* question.

pronto   *soon, quickly*

My friends who went to buy some peanut butter
Soon found me <u>**prone, toe**</u> broken, in the gutter.

puerta   *door*

Why do you let Po<u>**p wear Ta**</u>hiti sandals?
You've opened up the *door* to endless scandals.

puerto   *port, harbor*

They made Po<u>**p wear to**</u>bacco-colored shorts
While chasing after spies in foreign *ports*.

punto   *point*

When Ben's har<u>**poon to**</u>re up the joint
I guess the owner got the *point*.

Qq–Rr

queso   *cheese*

O.**K., so** you devoured the *cheese.*
Now down the milk, as Mom decrees.

quitar   *to leave*

Jane *left* the house in wrath, to use no more
The house **key Tar**zan kept above the door.

rama   *branch*

D**rama** struck the Hi-Lo Ranch
When Fred was felled by an oak-tree *branch.*

reclamar   *to claim, demand, complain*

Pa, **rake La Mar** across the coals:
He *claims* to win each time he bowls.

recto, –a   *straight*

Mama w**recked o**ld Oliver's Chevrolet.
The road was *straight* but he wouldn't get out of her way.

queso   *cheese*

O.**K., so** you devoured the *cheese*.
Now down the milk, as Mom decrees.

reinado　　　　*reign*

A spring **rain—ah! though** it's arriving late,
Will end the *reign* of drought throughout the state.

relucir　　　　*to glow, gleam, shine*

Ray, loose ear-rings fall and vanish in the snow,
But if I had some diamonds they'd never cease *to glow.*

rematar　　　　*to end, close, finish*

Ray, Ma targeted our school's decay.
She *ended* with a slap at PTA.

rey (m.)　　　　*king*

A **ray** of hope lights up the gloom:
The *King* has rented our front room.

roble (m.)　　　　*oak*

Roe blames Rob for cutting down the *oak*
Where for the last time our great preacher spoke.

ropa　　　　*clothing, clothes*

I'll **rope a** cow for leather *clothing*—
A job that fills my heart with loathing.

rostro　　　　*face, countenance, visage*

I'll feed your *face* with something really yummy:
A **roast ro**bust enough to fill your tummy.

ropa   *clothing, clothes*

I'll **rope a** cow for leather *clothing*—
A job that fills my heart with loathing.

_Ss_

salsa   _gravy, sauce_

Lieutenant **Sol sa**luted Colonel Davy:
"Sir, may I ask you how you made that _gravy?_"

sazón (m.)   _seasoning_

El**sa, Son**ya only tried, by reasoning,
To show that men, like food, improve with _seasoning._

según   _according to_

Men **say goon**s like you will have to go to school,
Although they never learn to live _according to_ a rule.

seguro   _sure, certain, safe_

The girls **say goo ro**lled out of the oven door.
I'm _sure_ we'll have to scrub the kitchen floor.

sentar   _to seat_

The general **sent Ar**my troops to save us
And barber chairs in which _to seat_ and shave us.

ser *to be (held)*

A **cer**emony ***will be*** held at seven
To celebrate the child's new life in heaven.

siempre *always*

You should **see Em pray** daily at the shrine.
When she gets home she ***always*** seems to shine.

silbar *to whistle*

Seal Barbara in blooms of thistle.
Just think how all the boys will ***whistle!***

sol (m.) *sun*

The **sole** objection under the ***sun***
I have to Nick: he's not much fun.

soltar *to loosen, untie*

The shoe-**sole Tar**zan once had thought so neat
Was loosened by the puddles on the street.

sucio, -a *dirty*

Can't **Sue see o**ver the window sill?
Her ***dirty*** laundry is out there still.

suegro *father-in-law*

Our garments **sway gro**tesquely on the line:
My child's, my mate's, my ***father-in-law***'s, and mine.

suerte (f.)   *luck*

I **swear ta**me pigs have all the *luck.*
They roll in mud and don't get stuck.

sumir   *to sink, plunge* (tr.)

Sue mirrors one of my most secret wishes:
To sink my body in the world of fishes
And never have to rise and do the dishes.

Tt

tapiz (m.)   *tapestry*

<u>Top Eas</u>ter hats this year are trimmed with bunnies
Cut from old *tapestries* and Sunday funnies.

tarea   *assignment, job, task*

Gre<u>ta, Ray a</u>pproves your new *assignment:*
To sell our shoes to women of refinement.

tedio   *boredom, tedium*

You need not s<u>**tay. The o**</u>nly thing you know
Is spreading *boredom* everywhere you go.

tela   *web, cloth, screen*

It's just a fairy <u>**tale a**</u> nanny told
About a magic *web* that turned to gold.

tenis (m.)   *tennis*

My <u>**tennie s**</u>plit while I was playing *tennis*
With unforgotten Sally, my old menace.

traer   *to bring*

Bring ex<u>**tra air**</u>; inflate his ego.
If you can't go, why not let me go?

tienda   *store*

You should see Aun**tie end a** fight
In Uncle's *store* on Saturday night.

tinta   *ink*

Teen taboos have kept us two apart,
But pen and *ink* may bring us heart to heart.

tirar   *to draw, pull, shoot*

Steer Arthur to the fire, and all together
We'll *draw* the curtains on the stormy weather.

tocar   *to play (a musical instrument); to touch*

I met Joe Bar**tow car**ting home a banjo.
I sneered and muttered, "*Play* it if you can, Joe!"

todo   *every*

I'm sure the villain trod upon my **toe**,
though *every*body swears it isn't so.

traer   *to bring*

Bring ex**tra air;** inflate his ego.
If you can't go, why not let me go?

tragar   *to swallow*

We'll send an ex**tra guar**d to Sleepy Hollow,
Though Rip van Winkle's yarn is hard *to swallow.*

trigo   *wheat*

Go plant the **tree. Go** sow the *wheat.*
For me—I'm off to join the fleet.

turista (m. or f.)   *tourist*

Tour east o' here a mile or two.
You'll see a *tourist's* dream come true.

Uu–Vv

uva *grape*

—He takes our horn of plenty and escapes!
—But then, he's left a **tuba** full of *grapes.*

vanidoso, –a *vain*

<u>**Bonnie, though so**</u> *vain* of being thin,
Has never learned to hold her stomach in.

ventoso, –a *windy*

<u>**Bent oh! so**</u> low in sleet and snow,
Over the *windy* hills we go.

ver *to see*

Two scenes that I can't **<u>bear</u>** *to see:*
Hans with you and Fritz with me.

viajar *to travel*

<u>**Be a har**</u>dy spirit! Don't unravel
Just because you don't much like *to travel.*

viaje (m.)   *trip*

<u>**Be ah! hay**</u>-fever-free this ***trip:***
Just take some pills to stop the drip.

vida   *life*

O clown, this has to <u>**be the** *life*</u> you chose,
Or else you wouldn't wear those silly clothes.

volar   *to fly*

A rain<u>**bow lar**</u>gely occupies the sky.
The dazzled birds can find no room ***to fly.***

voz (f.)   *voice*

Reginald's ***voice*** is the family's <u>**boast**</u>;
It pierces the night like the wail of a ghost.

Final Exam

How well have you learned the Spanish words you have studied in this book? The following short test will answer this question.

Each of the 20 jingles below contains the sounds of a Spanish word that you have learned from this book, but the jingles themselves you have not seen before. The jingles are constructed just like those in the vocabulary section. The English word is bold italic, but the Spanish word is not marked. See if you can find and underscore the consecutive syllables that approximate the sound of the Spanish word. (Remember that the bold italic verb may appear in a form other than the infinitive.)

When you have finished the test, look up the English words in the glossary to see if you got the right answers. If your answers are all correct, your score is 100; you can congratulate yourself on a considerable achievement. If you missed some of the questions, subtract 5 from 100 for each wrong answer. If you scored 80, you did all right. Below 80, you need to review a bit.

1.
He claims to be the *life* of the party.
To me he's only a stuck-up smarty.

2.
It's clear *to see* you rank a bit above me,
And I can bear to know you do not love me,
But surely that's no cause to push and shove me!

3.
Your lecture helped me elevate my thinking.
But our supply of bread and *honey*'s shrinking.

4.
The moon, Dolores, orbiting the *earth,*
Shines in Peoria as well as Perth.

5.
A tree goes "Ssssh" in the warm spring breeze,
And the *wheat* sways golden about my knees.

6.
You don't pay ordinary bills; and, *worse,*
Dismiss would-be collectors with a curse.

7.
Darling, you who have so much *to give,*
Give me the right to share the life you live.

8.

Dee a *day* in the shopping center sported.
When she went home, the girl was well escorted.

9.

My hen takes *people* into the barn,
Cackling over some egghead yarn.

10.

Pa, start up the motor, let's get zinging.
We'll sail *until* we hear the mermaids singing.

11.

I chose a room, May, though I knew
It's *humid,* and too small for two.

12.

Moe, though courteous, eyed me in a *way*
That made me think he wished I wouldn't stay.

13.

Nah, the April showers will never go away,
And *no one* here can hope to see the birds and
buds of May.

14.

Each noon Collette has lunch with all the frills,
But *never* thinks of picking up the bills.

15.

Ah, lay gray ferns within the airy nest
Where **happy,** but endangered, birdlings nest.

16.

A cola drink will make you brave
Enough to dive into a **wave.**

17.

Bob, a Chinese sage, long since averred:
"Confide your thoughts—but only to a **bird.**"

18.

Ah, Sue, luck failed you. But the skies are **blue.**
The storm will pass; and next time, so will you.

19.

By large expenditures in France
The clumsy fellow learned **to dance.**

20.

Your composition, stamped and sealed,
Fell in a pond in yonder **field.**

Glossary

English	Spanish
according to	según
account	cuenta
ad	aviso
advertisement	aviso
against	contra
agricultural	agrícola
all the way to	hasta
allow	dejar
although	aunque
always	siempre
anniversary	aniversario
another	otro
answer (v.)	contestar
anticipate	prever
appreciate	apreciar
arm (weapon)	arma
ask	pedir
ask for	pedir
assignment	tarea
atrocious	atroz
attend	asistir

English	Spanish
badly	mal
base (v.)	fundar
be (held)	ser
beard	barba
because	porque
begin to appear	asomar
bill (n.)	cuenta
bird	ave
bite (n.)	bocado
blue	azul
body	cuerpo
bone	hueso
boredom	tedio
boss	jefe
bow (weapon)	arco
box	caja
boy	mozo
brake (n.)	freno
branch	rama
bring	traer
brother	hermano
bull	buey
burden	cargo
but	pero
call (v.)	llamar
campus	campo
cap	gorra
capable	capaz

English	*Spanish*
celery	apio
certain	seguro
chain (n.)	cadena
cheese	queso
chew	mascar
chief	jefe
claim (v.)	reclamar
classroom	aula
climb	escalar
cloak	manto
close (v.)	rematar
cloth	tela
clothes	ropa
clothing	ropa
coarse	basto
come into view	asomar
commit	cometer
complain	reclamar
contempt	desprecio
countenance	figura, rostro
crime	delito
damp	húmedo
dance (v.)	bailar
danger	peligro
dawn	aurora
day	día
demand (v.)	reclamar
descend	bajar

English	*Spanish*
desire (v.)	desear
dessert	postre
direct (v.)	dirigir
dirty	sucio
disdain (n.)	desprecio
dizziness	mareo
dizzy spell	mareo
dog	perro
door	puerta
dough	masa
draw (v.)	tirar
drink (v.)	beber
drop (n.)	gota
dust (n.)	polvo
earth	mundo
eat	comer
egg yolk	gema
eight	ocho
elk	alce
end (v.)	rematar
escape (n.)	huida
every	todo
excuse (v.)	disculpar
face (n.)	cara, rostro
faithful	fiel
fall (v.)	caer

English	*Spanish*
fashion	moda
fast (n.)	ayuno
fat	gordo
father–in–law	suegro
fear (n.)	miedo
feed (v.)	alimentar
field	campo
fight (n.)	lucha, pelea
fight (v.)	luchar
figure (n.)	figura
fine (adv.)	bien
finger	dedo
finish (v.)	rematar
fleet (n.)	flota
flight	huída
fly (v.)	volar
foolish	bobo
foot	pie
for	para
foresee	prever
forget	olvidar
found (establish)	fundar
free (adj.)	libre
freeze	helar
gap	hueco
garden	huerto
garlic	ajo

English	*Spanish*
German	alemán
get off	bajar
give	dar
gleam (v.)	relucir
glow (v.)	relucir
go	ir
goat	cabra
good	bueno
good–bye	adiós
grape	uva
gravy	salsa
greet	acoger
guarantee (v.)	fiar
guide (n.)	guía
gun	arma
hand	mano
happy	alegre, feliz
harbor (n.)	puerto
harbor (v.)	acoger
haughty	altivo
have (aux.)	haber
head	cabeza
here	acá
high	alto
hole	hueco
homespun	basto
honey	miel

English	*Spanish*
hotel	hotel
human	humano
humid	húmedo
ill	enfermo
in order to	para
ink	tinta
insane	loco
isthmus	istmo
jail	cárcel
job	tarea
joy	gozo
junk	junco
(a Chinese ship)	
king	rey
landlord	amo
law	ley
lazy	perezoso
learn	aprender
leave	quitar
leave behind	dejar
less	menos
life	vida
little	pequeño
load (n.)	cargo

English	*Spanish*
look for	buscar
loosen	soltar
lose	perder
love (n.)	amor
low	bajo
loyal	fiel
luck	suerte
mad	loco
man	hombre
manner	manera
mantle	manto
March	marzo
meal	comida
meat	carne
merry	alegre
monkey	mono
moose	alce
more	más
mouthful	bocado
much	mucho
museum	museo
mute	mudo
name	nombre
nausea	asco
never	jamás, nunca
no one	nadie

English	*Spanish*
oak	roble
ocean	océano
oppress	oprimir
orchard	huerto
ostrich	avestruz
other	otro
outside	afuera
ox	buey
painter	pintor
pale	pálido
pay (v.)	pagar
pen	pluma
people	gente
pillar	poste
pit	pozo
place (v.)	poner
platform	andén
play (an instrument)	tocar
pluck	pelar
plunge	sumir
point (n.)	punto
pole	poste
politely	atentamente
port	puerto
post (n.)	poste
pound	libra

English	*Spanish*
prepare	aparejar
present, be	asistir
press (v.)	oprimir
pretty	bonito
previous	previo
prick (v.)	picar
prior	previo
proud	altivo
pull	tirar
pull out (hair)	pelar
quickly	pronto
race (n.)	carrera
reach (a place)	alcanzar
receive	acoger
reign (n.)	reinado
reply (v.)	contestar
repugnance	asco
request (v.)	pedir
rig (v.)	aparejar
rock (v.)	mecer
run	correr
safe (adj.)	seguro
sauce	salsa
save	ahorrar
scale (v.)	escalar

English	*Spanish*
scream (v.)	gritar
screen	tela
search (n.)	busca
seasoning	sazón
seat (v.)	sentar
see	ver
seek	buscar
sell on credit	fiar
set (v.)	poner
shape (n.)	figura
shine (v.)	relucir
shoot	tirar
short	bajo
shout (v.)	gritar
sick	enfermo
sidewalk	acera
silent	mudo
silly	bobo
sing	cantar
sink (v. tr.)	sumir
skate (v.)	patinar
sleep (v.)	dormir
small	pequeño
so	así
sock (n.)	calcetín
some	alguno
song	canto
soon	pronto

English	*Spanish*
spin (v.)	hilar
split (v.)	hender
squeeze	apretar
steel	acero
steer (n.)	buey
steer (v.)	dirigir
sting (v.)	picar
stop (v.)	parar
store (n.)	almacén, tienda
straight	recto
struggle (v.)	luchar
sugar	azúcar
suitcase	maleta
sun	sol
sure	seguro
swallow (v.)	tragar
swimming	natación
swing (v.)	mecer
tall	alto
tapestry	tapiz
task	tarea
tedium	tedio
tennis	tenis
though	aunque
thousand	mil
thus	así
toe	dedo

English	*Spanish*
touch (v.)	tocar
tourist	turista
travel (v.)	viajar
trip (n.)	viaje
trust (v.)	fiar
Tuesday	martes
turn off	apagar
untie	soltar
until	hasta
vain	vanidoso
visage	rostro
voice	voz
waiter	mozo
wall	muro
want (v.)	desear
wave (n.)	ola
way	manera, modo
weapon	arma
web	tela
well (adv.)	bien
well (n.)	pozo
wheat	trigo
whistle (v.)	silbar
wide	ancho
windy	ventoso

English	*Spanish*
wish (v.)	desear
word	palabra
world	mundo
worse	peor
write down	anotar
yellow	amarillo